Highlights
Hidden Pictures

Silly Sticker Stories

Easter Tales

HIGHLIGHTS PRESS

Honesdale, Pennsylvania

Create your own silly story!

Each Hidden Pictures® puzzle in this book comes with a story for you to finish. Use the tear-out sticker sheets to start puzzling!

Here's what you do:

1 Find a hidden object.

2 Peel the sticker.

At the Egg Plant
pages 4–5

hockey stick • paper clip • harmonica • horseshoe • dustpan • flying saucer

mushroom • waffle • ladle • straw • lollipop • ruler

My First Hare Cut
pages 6–7

magnet • top hat • binoculars • knitted hat • paintbrush • teacup

Of Bee I Sing
pages 8–9

party hat • ruler • mitten • sailboat • pencil • olive

snail • lollipop • bell • paper clip • fork • glove

Bunny Hops
pages 10–11

snake • leaf • snowman • sock • thread • glove

ice-cream cone • sailboat • plate • lock

At the Egg Plant

I love my _____! Sure, some days _____ asleep on my living-room _____ be_____ even taken off my floppy _____. Still, that's the way it is with seasonal work. Usually I can take a long, leisurely _____ at Bunita's _____ Café. But from Christmas to Easter, I barely have a minute to grab even a handful of crispy _____ snacks before I have to get back to the assembly line. I'm the manager, and I have to keep a watchful _____ on my crew. No one has ever let me forget the time Jack Rabbit fell into the _____ full of purple _____. For weeks after, everyone called him "The Grape _____!" But the long hours are worth it to ensure that a colorful hand-painted _____ winds up in everyone's Easter _____. As I like to say, "I make my living by dyeing!"

BONUS: Can you find the button, orange, and book?

Art by Neil Numberman

4

5

Contents

3

Place it in the story.

4

Read aloud and giggle!

At the Egg Plant

I love my _____! Sure, some days I come home so tired that I fall

asleep on my living-room _____ before I've even taken off my

floppy _____. Still, that's the way it is with seasonal work. Usually I

can take a long, leisurely _____ at Bunita's _____ Café. But

from Christmas to Easter, I barely have a minute to grab even a handful

of crispy _____ snacks before I have to get back to the assembly

line. I'm the manager, and I have to keep a watchful _____ on

my crew. No one has ever let me forget the time Jack Rabbit fell into

the _____ full of purple _____. For weeks after, everyone

called him "The Grape _____!" But the long hours are worth it to

ensure that a colorful hand-painted _____ winds up in everyone's

Easter _____. As I like to say, "I make my living by dyeing!"

BONUS: Can you find the button, orange, and book?

My First Hare Cut

"Just a little off the top, please," I said, trying to sound as calm as a

floating _____ on a spring breeze. The next day would be my first

time hopping down The _____ Trail. I wanted to look my best.

So I was really nervous when Mr. _____ pulled out a super-long

_____ and sharpened it on a leather _____. Luckily, he put

that down and grabbed scissors instead. With each snip, I was sure I'd

end up as bald as a hard-boiled _____! To make it worse, the

Hedgehog twins kept giggling and whispering about my _____ as

they waited with their mom. Finally the barber rubbed a glob of

gooey _____ through my _____, then handed me a big,

round _____ for a look. The spiky _____ wasn't my style,

but at least I wasn't a hairless _____!

BONUS: Can you find the straw, snake, nail, and pitcher?

Of Bee I Sing

We'd rehearsed for the annual _____ Town Spring _____

Concert for weeks. So I wasn't exactly thrilled when Ms. Walsh picked

me at the last minute to wear the _____ T-shirt and put the bright

orange _____ around my _____. But it was too late to get

out of it. We had just started singing "In your Easter _____, with

all the frills upon it," when I heard this buzzing sound, like a supersonic

_____ soaring past my _____. At first I thought it was

Jimmy Rivera's sore _____ acting up again. Yesterday, he'd sounded

just like a rusty old _____ revving up. But then this ginormous

yellow _____ dive-bombed me! I jumped back just in time. But

wouldn't you know it? Our concert ended with the song "Be My Little

Baby Bumble _____"!

BONUS: Can you find the banana?

Bunny Hops

Recess is more than just playtime at _____ Heights Middle School. It's

everyone's chance to show off their latest fancy _____ tricks. They

just might get one of us into the Long-Earred _____ Olympics or the

_____-Roping Hall of Fame some day. Eddie is pretty sure he has a

winner with his reverse _____ aerial. Bonnie is practicing her lucky

_____'s-foot move. For months now, I've been working on my double

side-to-side _____. But every time I swing my _____ to the

left, I wind up spinning to the right and landing flat on my furry _____!

Today I got so tangled up that I looked like one giant messy _____ of

yarn. Once the _____ rings, though, we will each hop as quick as a

bunny back into the school. Nobody wants our principal, Mr. _____,

to think that we're skipping class!

BONUS: Can you find the bowl?

Art by Tamara Petrosino

Nothing but Nest

Our parents had a big _____ for us: we were going to Uncle Tim's

_____ for Easter! When we arrived, our uncle gave us each a

wooden _____. I looked inside mine. "It's empty!" I said.

He chuckled. "You can't color Easter eggs without eggs. The nearest

_____ is fifty miles away, so you'll have to collect each

_____ yourselves." Then he showed us to the _____ coop.

The hens didn't seem too happy to see us. One flew up onto the

_____. Another flapped its _____ at my brother and

squawked like a broken _____ with all the _____ squeezed

out of it. But then things calmed down, and we could reach into each

straw-filled _____. When I handed my full _____

to Uncle Tim, I asked, "Next time, can we just color *chocolate* eggs?"

BONUS: Can you find the banana?

Art by Mike Dammer

13

The Master at Work

You must make an appointment years in advance with Leonardo da

_____, the world-famous Easter-egg painter. Each of his designs is

a one-of-a-kind _____ of art! He creates patterns with a squiggly

_____ here and a polka-dot _____ there. But if inspired,

he will draw a complete _____ right before your eyes. Once he

painted a Hawaiian _____ that looked so real you could smell the

_____ lotion! So when I handed him my jumbo-size _____,

I wondered what special _____ he would make just for me. But

when he'd finished, I blurted out, "_____ ! My egg is still white!"

"Not at all!" Leonardo explained. "In science class, we learned that white

light is an amazing _____ of ALL the colors. So as you can

see, I used every paint in my _____!"

BONUS: Can you find the eyeglasses, candle, and ring?

Mail-Order Rab-Bot

Roger and I had a genius idea! To win the Easter _____ hunt

this year, we'd use a little technological _____. We figured a

_____-controlled device could easily sniff out even the most well-

hidden _____. So we sent away for the Deluxe _____

Rab-Bot 2000. When the big cardboard _____ arrived, though,

we saw we'd have to put the _____ together ourselves! So we laid

all the parts out on the living-room _____, grabbed a long-handled

_____, and started assembling. We had just enough time to get to

the _____ before the hunt started. As our creation raced around

the field, we knew something was wrong. Roger groaned, "Jessica, I think

we put the high-voltage _____ in upside down." He was right. So

we didn't win the contest. But later we made a lot of _____ soup!

BONUS: Can you find the pitcher, crown, golf club, cane, pencil,
envelope, hairpin, can, teacup, bowl, and ruler?

Art by Bill Golliher

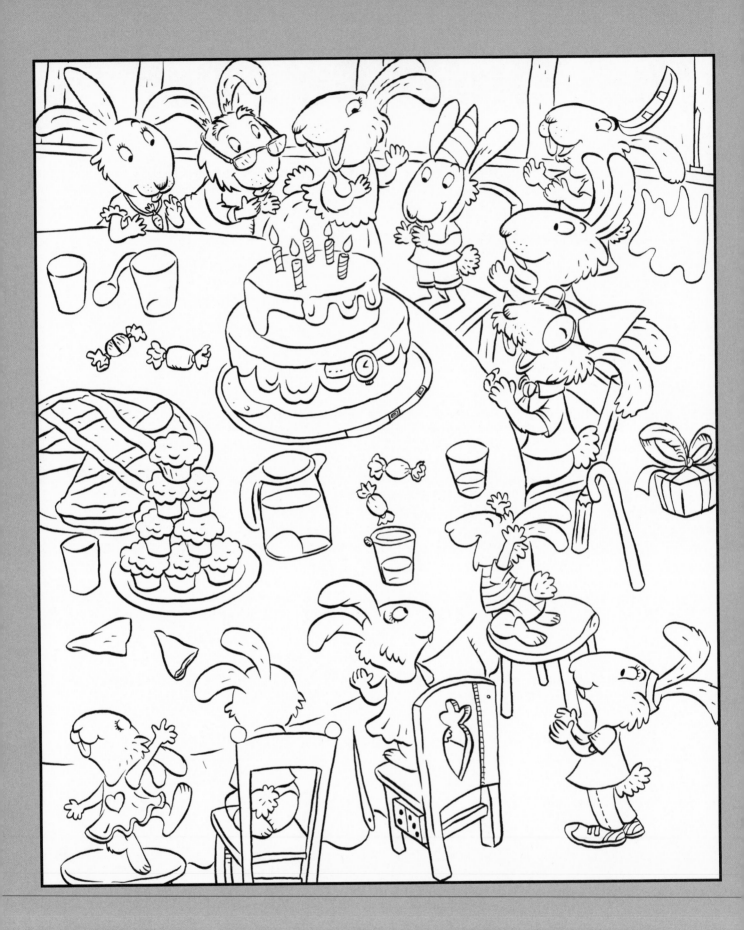

Favorite Party Ever!

My birthday is my favorite _____ of the year. So it was even more

awesome that, this year, it fell on Easter—my favorite _____!

What could be better? A surprise _____ with all my friends! Mom

and Dad had made my favorite foods, like _____ butter-and-jelly

muffins, pepperoni-and-_____ pizza, and a big _____ of

ice-cold _____. We played my favorite games, too: Pin the Cotton

_____ on the _____ and Duck, Duck, _____! Just

when I thought this birthday couldn't be any more perfect, my parents

brought out the special dessert that Grandma had baked and frosted

with my favorite color icing—_____. And of course, the dessert

was my very favorite kind: a four-layer _____ cake!

BONUS: Can you find the ring, belt, ruler, canoe, pencil, and needle?

Art by Nuno Alexandre Vieira

19

Up in the Air

Each year, we Easter bunnies bounce door-to-door to deliver a treat-

stuffed _____ to everyone. And each year, my feet are so sore

that I have to soak them in a steaming _____ of hot _____

as soon as I get back to my cozy _____. Then Amelia Earhart

came up with a brilliant _____: Why hop when you can fly? Amelia

had gone to the International _____ Fiesta in Albuquerque last

October. As she watched each colorful _____ float past a puffy

_____, she realized they looked just like decorated eggs. So she

suggested we use "air mail"! We did tests to be sure we had the right

size _____ to tie on to each packed _____. That was as

tricky as juggling a squirming _____! But we finally got it right. All

the packages landed safely—and not one scrambled _____!

BONUS: Can you find the mallet and mushroom?

Hidden Treasures

"Welcome one and all to the Springfield _____ Scramble at

_____ Park! Before we begin, I must go over a few _____

rules. Number 1: Watch your step! You wouldn't want to squish a

hidden _____, would you? Number 2: No running through the

_____ garden! You won't find anything there anyway. Number 3:

Don't bother looking in the _____ cans either. You'll see nothing

but a stinky _____. Number 4: Please don't eat what you find!

The eggs have been out in the hot _____ all morning and you

could wind up with a _____-ache. Besides, they're made of

plastic. Number 5: When the _____ blows, return to the main

_____ for the final count. Number 6: Have fun! No matter what,

everyone will win at least one prize: a solid chocolate _____ !"

BONUS: Can you find the moon, paintbrush, glove, eyeglasses,
teacup, ring, hockey stick, bell, crown, candle, mallet, fork, and spoon?

Art by Chuck Galey

First Rehearsal

We, the Mossville School Marching _____, were chosen from

among hundreds of performers from across the _____ to lead

off the 36th Annual Bugburg _____ Parade! Our first practice

got off to a shaky start, though, when Adam discovered that a fuzzy

_____ had made a nest in his jazz _____; he had to clean

it with a big wet soapy _____. Andrea was excited to try out her

shiny new _____, but the keys kept sticking and it sounded like a

wheezy old _____ with a head cold. Anita Firefly swooped in for

a listen and nearly collided with Anthony and his booming _____.

Then a gusty _____ blew the sheet music off the conductor's

_____, and we lost our _____. Luckily, we worked the

bugs out, and now we're ready to march and play!

BONUS: Can you find the number 7 and high-heeled shoe?

Hats On!

Let's be honest. When Ms. Eloise opened her fancy _____

shop, Eloise's House of _____ Wear, many of us in town

didn't expect it to do well. Who wears a frilly _____ or a

feathered _____ or a flouncy _____ anymore? Then the

mayor announced that he'd be handing out a spectacular, stupendous,

splendid _____ to whomever marched in the Easter parade

wearing the most spectacular, stupendous, splendid _____. So you

can imagine how busy Eloise's store was then! Folks were snapping up

a bouquet-topped _____ or a bow-tied _____. The day of

the parade, not one _____ heading down _____ Street was

uncovered. I couldn't believe it when I won! But guess what the prize

was? A frilly, feathered, flouncy _____ from Eloise's shop!

BONUS: Can you find the pear, button, lollipop,
teacup, pencil, and apple?

27

Art by Lyn Martin

Grandma's Gifts

As we waved goodbye to Grandma, I was already thinking about what

a great time we'd had. For Easter dinner, she made her famous creamed

_____ with cheesy _____ and a juicy baked _____

that was as humongous as a prehistoric _____. Then she sent

us on a treasure hunt! She gave us each a list of clues that would lead

to a gift. I found a jigsaw _____, a jangly _____, and a jelly

_____. But there was still one clue left: "Paws before you find the

*purr*fect prize." I was stumped! So I combed the whole house again,

looking under the _____, on top of the _____, even inside

the _____. The whole time, Grandma's cat, _____, just lay on

the rug, purring. Finally, I understood. I gently lifted up the cat's paws, and

there was the final prize: a glow-in-the-dark _____!

BONUS: Can you find the fishing pole and shovel?

Puddle Jumpers

Today was supposed to be the first _____ of the season for

our track-and-_____ team, the Springfield _____ Tigers.

Instead, we were rained out! Alex and I kept texting each other, adding

_____ emojis at the end of each _____. "I was sure I was

going to win the standing _____ jump today," she wrote. "I've

been practicing by leaping over the widest _____ I could find."

I texted back, "I still need to work on my 50-_____ dash." Then

I had an idea. "Put on your yellow _____ and meet me at the

_____ in five minutes." When we got there, we had the place

to ourselves. I raced up and down the cement _____ while Alex

leaped over the soggy _____. Then we each practiced

a victory dance in the biggest puddle we could find!

On the March

"Ladybugs and Gentlepests, welcome to the 36th Annual Bugburg

_____ Parade. As your mayor, I'd like to thank the sponsor of

this amazing event: Anthill Farms, our local orchard and bakery that

makes a tasty _____-flavored _____ that will melt in your

_____! Of course, the incredible inflatable _____ is courtesy

of _____ Troop 24. And finally, all the way from Mossville is the

very talented _____ band, whose _____ bus nearly broke

down on the road. It seems a slimy _____ had crawled into the

engine's _____. But luckily the band still made it on time! Now

remember, yours truly will be giving free _____-and-

buggy rides after the parade. You also won't want to miss

tonight's rock 'n' roll _____, starring The Beetles!"

Good Skates

The first day of spring always brings us out to _____ Park to

show off our mad _____ skills. But this year there was a special

_____-only course that wound all through the park. We were

as happy as a chirping _____ with a juicy _____! Allie Gator

was kicking it with his goofy-foot _____. Francesco Fox flipped

a 360 mega-_____ while belting out his favorite song, "Magic

_____ Ride." What we didn't know was that the path was still

under construction. When we all shot around a curve, we saw a giant

churning _____ up ahead. As we swerved to avoid it, Francesco

flew into a thorny _____. Allie went headfirst into the mushy

_____. Somehow, I managed to ride up a skinny _____ and

sailed over it. "Cool!" I shouted afterward. "Let's do that again!"

BONUS: Can you find the envelope, domino,
button, wishbone, glove, crown, colander, and thread?

Alien Landing

We weren't quite sure what it was at first. Bobby heard a strange

_____ and flew down from his _____ to investigate. Once

he laid eyes on that colossal _____, he started buzzing about it.

"I'm sure it landed from another _____," he said. "I'll bet inside

is a triple-headed _____ with a scaly _____ and a huge

jagged _____!" Ignatius knocked on the outside, then jumped back.

"Whoa! I felt something stomp like an angry _____!" Felicia put

her ear to it. "Something's growling in there like a hungry _____,"

she said. Finally, Petey walked over. (You'd think someone with 100 legs

would move faster, but he's as slow as a dripping _____.) "Oh, it's

just a missing _____!" he explained. We were disappointed. We

really wanted to see that triple-headed, angry, hungry _____!

BONUS: Can you find the needle and mitten?

Art by Neil Numberman

37

Cabbage Patch

We O'Hares do things a bit differently. Unlike our neighbors, we've

never planted a carrot _____. You won't find even one skinny

orange _____ on our farm. To us, nothing beats a fat, leafy

_____ of cabbage. It's a much more versatile _____! You

can slice it into strips with a sharp _____ and mix it with a creamy

_____ to make _____-slaw. Or shred it and soak it in a salty

_____ for days, then use it to top off a grilled _____. You

can even fill the big leaves with chopped _____ and wrap each up

into a mouthwatering _____ roll! Yum! And when our neighbors

get tired of eating carrots day after day, we invite them over for dinner

and serve all our favorite cabbage dishes. The best one

is dessert: _____-cabbage pudding!

BONUS: Can you find the banana, pie, and ring?

Choosy Shoes

Every year, I have to pick out a new spring _____. My parents

say that's because I'm growing as tall as a rubber _____ in the

_____ jungle. "And don't you want to look as handsome as a royal

_____ when we go to Grandpa's for Easter?" they added. So I

tried on every _____ in the store until I found one that fit. Then

I had to get a new shirt and even a pin-striped _____. The last

thing was a pair of new shoes. I really wanted the leather _____

boots—I could see myself on a bucking _____ and lassoing a

wild _____! The store also carried the latest _____-Rocket

sneakers, just like my sports hero, "_____" Jackson, wears! But my

parents said, "No way!" Then I spotted the perfect pair for Easter. Even

Grandpa loved my furry, long-eared _____ shoes!

Missed a Spot

This _____ holiday, my parents put me in charge of helping my little

brother and sister decorate every last _____ in the refrigerator.

Luckily, I think decorating eggs is even more fun than opening a brand

new _____ on Christmas morning or dressing up as a _____

on Halloween. I couldn't wait to show them how to use the _____

stencils so we could add a colorful _____ and _____ design

to the eggs. Before long we were painting a poufy _____ here and

a sparkly _____ there. We didn't even notice when Ralphy dipped

his paws in the purple _____ and smeared it all over the entire

_____. Mom wasn't too happy about that. But by the end of the

day, we had the most egg-cellently decorated _____ in the

entire neighborhood! (And the biggest mess to clean up.)

BONUS: Can you find the mallet, candle, and flag?

Art by Mary Sullivan

43

Garden Variety

I was all set for the _____-growing competition at the state fair in

Veggieville. My entry would be the biggest, most beautiful _____.

I had planted the seed in the sunniest _____ in my garden. As it

sprouted, I pulled each pesky _____ that sprung up around it. I had

even sent away for a super-nutritious _____ mixture, made from the

smooshed-up _____ of a slightly overripe _____ and applied it

every day. Now my entry was perfect! But I couldn't sleep the night before

the contest. I kept tossing and turning like a buttermilk _____ on

a sizzling _____. That morning, I was too excited to have my usual

breakfast of Frosted _____ Nuggets with a sliced-up _____.

Then by the time the judging started . . . well, I didn't get the blue ribbon.

But my entry did get an award for Chewiest _____!

BONUS: Can you find the cherries?

Answers

▼ Front Cover

▼ Page 4

▼ Page 6

▼ Page 8

▼ Page 10

▼ Page 12

▼ Page 14

▼ Page 16

▼ Page 18

Answers

▼Page 20

▼Page 22

▼Page 24

▼Page 26

▼Page 28

▼Page 30

▼Page 32

▼Page 34

▼Page 36

Answers

▼Page 38

▼Page 40

▼Page 42

▼Page 44

At the Egg Plant
pages 4–5

 hockey stick
 paper clip
 harmonica
 horseshoe
 dustpan
 flying saucer

 mushroom
 waffle
 ladle
 straw
 lollipop
 ruler

My First Hare Cut
pages 6–7

 magnet
 top hat
 binoculars
 knitted hat
 paintbrush
 teacup

 party hat
 ruler
 mitten
 sailboat
 pencil
 olive

Of Bee I Sing
pages 8–9

 snail
 lollipop
 bell
 paper clip
 fork
 glove

 ice-cream cone
 leaf
 snowman
 sock
 thread
 lock

Bunny Hops
pages 10–11

 snake
 sailboat
 plate
 feather
 kite
 glove

 seashell
 ruler
 sock
 candle
 bell
 mushroom

Nothing but Nest
pages 12–13

 flag
 fork
 flashlight
 fly
 flower
 fish

 football
 fishhook
 ruler
 pencil
 toothbrush
 caterpillar

The Master at Work
pages 14–15

 wristwatch
 wishbone
 wooden shoe
 golf club
 elf's hat
 fishbowl

 canoe
 snake
 mug
 lollipop
 tack
 key

Mail-Order Rab-Bot
pages 16–17

 umbrella
 mushroom
 fish
 cupcake
 hockey stick
 olive

 comb
 boomerang
 mitten
 ladle
 paper airplane
 fried egg

Favorite Party Ever!
pages 18–19

 wristwatch
 domino
 moon
 nail
 slipper
 ghost

 sailboat
 snake
 sock
 acorn
 bell
 feather

Up in the Air
pages 20–21

book	flashlight	pie	teacup	domino	fish
peanut	thimble	sailboat	acorn	drum	crayon

Hidden Treasures
pages 22–23

ladder	book	cupcake	comb	screwdriver	mushroom
ice-cream cone	flashlight	lollipop	lighthouse	apple	butterfly

First Rehearsal
pages 24–25

trowel	adhesive bandage	golf club	envelope	lollipop	saltshaker
hourglass	doughnut	baby's bottle	arrowhead	toothbrush	paintbrush

Hats On!
pages 26–27

carrot	sailboat	seashell	candy cane	banana	lemon
paintbrush	ice-cream bar	cinnamon bun	slipper	light bulb	toothbrush

Grandma's Gifts
pages 28–29

taco	hockey stick	carrot	pie	key	book
toothbrush	fork	bell	pizza	candle	ice-cream bar

Puddle Jumpers
pages 30–31

snow cone	test tube	game piece	chicken drumstick	lemon	pie
broccoli	fish	domino	spoon	heart	light bulb

On the March
pages 32–33

paintbrush	fishhook	baby's bottle	broom	lollipop	fried egg
bell	ruler	sock	banana	teapot	pencil

Good Skates
pages 34–35

watermelon	football	lollipop	bowling ball	heart	cookie
magnet	golf club	belt	doughnut	broccoli	carrot

9928-04 © Highlights for Children

Alien Landing
pages 36–37

 scissors handbag teacup sock heart kite

 ring tennis racket crown straw button pie

Cabbage Patch
pages 38–39

 baseball bat seashell fish moon  paintbrush thread

 tennis racket ladder mitten canoe lemon cake

Choosy Shoes
pages 40–41

 banana hairbrush paintbrush magnifying glass nail belt

 frog leaf ladder canoe bell flag

Missed a Spot
pages 42–43

 toothbrush doughnut pencil worm sailboat banana

 pizza glove shoe magnet  saucepan mushroom

Garden Variety
pages 44–45

 football  turtle yo-yo fish  duck drumstick

 bowling pin pair of pants baseball cap ladle  rolling pin bat

Write your own
silly sticker story!
Use markers to
create your own
stickers.